Yellow Animals

Melissa Stewart

Enslow Elementary

an imprint of

Enslow Publishers, Inc.

40 Industrial Road
Box 398
Berkeley Heights, NJ 07922
USA

http://www.enslow.com

Enslow Elementary, an imprint of Enslow Publishers, Inc.
Enslow Elementary® is a registered trademark of Enslow Publishers, Inc.

Library of Congress Cataloging-in-Publication Data
Stewart, Melissa.
Yellow animals / Melissa Stewart.
p. cm. — (All about a rainbow of animals)
Includes bibliographical references and index.
Summary: "Introduces pre-readers to simple concepts about yellow animals using short sentences and repetition of words"—Provided by publisher.
ISBN 978-0-7660-3997-1 (alk. paper)
1. Animals—Color—Juvenile literature. 2. Yellow—Juvenile literature. I. Title.
QL767.S758 2012
590—dc23
2011027250

Future editions:
Paperback ISBN 978-1-4644-0045-2
ePUB ISBN 978-1-4645-0952-0
PDF ISBN 978-1-4645-0952-7

Printed in China
012012 Leo Paper Group, Heshan City, Guangdong, China
10 9 8 7 6 5 4 3 2 1

To Our Readers: We have done our best to make sure all Internet Addresses in this book were active and appropriate when we went to press. However, the author and the publisher have no control over and assume no liability for the material available on those Internet sites or on other Web sites they may link to. Any comments or suggestions can be sent by e-mail to comments@enslow.com or to the address on the back cover.

Photo Credits: Shutterstock.com
Cover Photo: Shutterstock.com

Note to Parents and Teachers

Help pre-readers get a jumpstart on reading. These lively stories introduce simple concepts with repetition of words and short simple sentences. Photos and illustrations fill the pages with color and effectively enhance the text. Free Educator Guides are available for this series at www.enslow.com. Search for the *All About a Rainbow of Animals* series name.

Contents

Words to Know

butterfly

monkey

spider

yellow snake

yellow spider

yellow monkey

yellow bird

yellow fish

yellow frog

yellow butterfly

yellow bee

owl with yellow eyes

yellow animals

Read More

Jenkins, Steve. *Living Color*. Boston: Houghton Mifflin, 2007.

Whitehouse, Patricia. *Colors We Eat: Yellow Foods*. Chicago: Heinemann, 2004.

Web Sites

Animal Colors
http://www.highlightskids.com/Science/Stories/SS1000_animalColors.asp

Animal Printable Coloring Pages
http://thecoloringspot.com/animals-coloring-pages/

Index

Guided Reading Level: A
Guided Reading Leveling System is based on the guidelines recommended by Fountas and Pinnell.

Word Count: 22